Collins

TREASURE HOUSE

Pupil Book 3

Spelling Skills

Authors: Sarah Snashall and Chris Whitney

HarperCollins
PUBLISHERS
Since 1817

William Collins' dream of knowledge for all began with the publication of his first book in 1819.

A self-educated mill worker, he not only enriched millions of lives, but also founded a flourishing publishing house. Today, staying true to this spirit, Collins books are packed with inspiration, innovation and practical expertise. They place you at the centre of a world of possibility and give you exactly what you need to explore it.

Collins. Freedom to teach.

Published by Collins
An imprint of HarperCollins*Publishers*
The News Building
1 London Bridge Street
London
SE1 9GF

Browse the complete Collins catalogue at
www.collins.co.uk

10 9 8 7 6 5 4 3 2 1

ISBN 978-0-00-823654-0

British Library Cataloguing in Publication Data

A Catalogue record for this publication is available from the British Library

Publishing Director: Lee Newman
Publishing Manager: Helen Doran
Senior Editor: Hannah Dove
Project Manager: Emily Hooton
Authors: Sarah Snashall and Chris Whitney
Development Editor: Jessica Marshall
Copy-editor: Gaynor Spry
Proofreader: Tracy Thomas
Cover design and artwork: Amparo Barrera and Ken Vail Graphic Design
Internal design concept: Amparo Barrera
Typesetter: Jouve India Private Ltd
Illustrations: Beatriz Castro, Jacqui Davis, Eva Morales, Dante Ginevra, David Pavon, Aptara and QBS
Production Controller: Rachel Weaver

Printed and bound by Grafica Veneta S.p.A.

Contents

Adding suffixes beginning with vowels to words of more than one syllable

When you add a suffix starting with a vowel to a word of more than one syllable that ends in a vowel and a consonant, the spelling rule depends on whether the last syllable is stressed or not. If the last syllable is stressed, double the final consonant. For example: **gar**den + **er** = gardener, but be**gin** + **er** = begi**nn**er.

Get started

Copy and complete the chart by sorting these words into two groups. One has been done for you.

1. listened
2. listener
3. gardener
4. forgotten
5. watering
6. gardening
7. beginner
8. upsetting

Consonant not doubled	Consonant doubled
listened	

Try these

Copy and correct these sentences. Underline the misspelt word that you have corrected. One has been done for you.

1. Janice prefered chocolate to ice cream.

   Answer: *Janice preferred chocolate to ice cream.*

2. Ada had forgoten to buy a card for her mum.
3. Danu's teacher is transfering him from Class 1 to Class 2.
4. Kay was begining to enjoy tennis.
5. Ms Hardcastle presentted the school prizes.

Now try these

Copy and complete the sentences by choosing the correct spelling of each word. One has been done for you.

1. Pandora knew that she should not have ______________ the box. (openned / opened)

   Answer: *Pandora knew that she should not have opened the box.*

2. It was ______________ for us to go into the forest by the school. (forbidden / forbiden)
3. Frida ______________ carefully to the teacher's instructions. (listenned / listened)
4. Jo ______________ not joining the cricket team at the start of term. (regreted / regretted)
5. Hanes enjoyed playing the flute, but he was only a ______________. (beginner / begginner)

The /i/ sound spelt y

In some words, the letter **y** is said as if it were an **i**. For example, the **y** in g**y**m sounds like the **i** in r**i**m. Here are some other words that follow this pattern:

- s**y**rup
- cr**y**stal

For these words, we spell the /i/ sound with a letter **y**.

Get started

Copy the words, then underline the **/i/** sound spelt **y**. One has been done for you.

1. gym

Answer: gym

2. myth

3. syrup

4. Egypt

5. crystal

6. pyramids

7. oxygen

8. typical

Try these

Copy the sentences and underline the words in which the **/i/** sound is spelt **y**. One has been done for you.

1. I poured some syrup onto my porridge.

   Answer: *I poured some syrup onto my porridge.*

2. My brother was pulling a funny face in the picture – it was typical of him!
3. Sal came up from underwater and took a big breath of oxygen.
4. The house with the yellow door was mysterious and old.
5. The glittering crystal glasses were on a silver tray.
6. Naveed's family is flying all the way to Egypt on holiday.

Now try these

Copy and complete the sentences by choosing the correct spelling of each word. One has been done for you.

1. The doctor asked me about my ______________. (simptoms / symptoms)

   Answer: *The doctor asked me about my symptoms.*

2. The story was about a ______________ beast with wings. (mythical / mithical)
3. Carin's jumper has the school ______________ on it. (symbol / simbol)
4. Jeremy was always ______________ in the shower. (singing / synging)
5. The distant land was ruled by a cruel ______________. (king / kyng)

The /u/ sound spelt ou

In some words, the letters **ou** are said as if they were a **u**. For example, the **ou** in t**ou**ch sounds like the **u** in m**u**ch. Some other words that follow this pattern are y**ou**ng and d**ou**ble.

Get started

Copy and complete the chart by sorting these words into two groups: words where **ou** stands for the **/u/** sound and words where it doesn't. One has been done for you.

1. young
2. cousin
3. count
4. mouth
5. noun
6. trouble
7. pound
8. double

ou spells **/u/**	**ou** doesn't spell **/u/**
young	

Try these

Copy and complete the sentences, then underline the words in which the letters **ou** make the **/u/** sound. One has been done for you.

1. My younger brother is out playing with his friends.

   Answer: *My younger brother is out playing with his friends.*

2. The new house is in the countryside.
3. Juan's cousin won an award – he was so proud of her!
4. There are a couple of clouds in the sky.
5. To score a point, just touch the ball to the ground.
6. If I do chores, I can double my two pounds pocket money.

Now try these

Copy and complete the sentences by choosing the correct spelling of each word. One has been done for you.

1. The married ______________ went on their honeymoon. (cuple / couple)

   Answer: *The married couple went on their honeymoon.*

2. I was in a good mood, so I was ______________ all the way to school. (humming / houmming)
3. Mr McCrury will ______________ us if we're late! (punish / pounish)
4. Jeni hopes she has the ______________ to sing on the stage. (currage / courage)
5. Patti fell and scraped her knee on the ______________ step. (rugh / rough)

The prefixes dis- and mis-

The prefix **dis–** normally means **not**. For example: **dis** + agree = **dis**agree.

The prefix **mis–** normally means **badly** or **incorrectly**. For example: **mis** + spell = **mis**spell.

Sometimes we use the prefixes **dis–** and **mis–** when there is not a clear root word.

Get started

Copy these words, then underline the prefixes. One has been done for you.

1. disbelief

Answer: <u>dis</u>belief

2. mislead

3. disappear

4. mistreat

5. discomfort

6. misplace

7. disobey

8. misunderstand

Try these

Copy the words below, separating the prefix and root word. One has been done for you.

1. misfortune

   Answer: *mis / fortune*

2. disallow
3. disagreement
4. disadvantage
5. mishear
6. disobedient

Now try these

Copy and complete the sentences by choosing the correct spelling of each word. One has been done for you.

1. Dasu and Ben never ________ on which game to play. (disagreed / dis-agreed)

   Answer: *Dasu and Ben never disagreed on which game to play.*

2. Finn was ________________ with the football result. (dissappointed / disappointed)
3. Amelie ________________ the question. (misheard / missheard)
4. Grace was ________________ about how much chocolate she'd had. (dishonest / dis-honest)
5. He made the cards ________________ in a puff of smoke! (dis-appear / disappear)

The prefixes in–, ir–, im– and il–

The prefix **in–** is used to mean **not**. When you add **in–** to a root word, you do not change the spelling of the root word. But sometimes you do have to change the spelling of **in–**.

If you add **in–** to a root word beginning with **l**, **in–** becomes **il–**.

If you add **in–** to a root word beginning with **m** or **p**, **in–** becomes **im–**.

If you add **in–** to a root word beginning with **r**, **in–** becomes **ir–**.

Get started

Copy these words, then underline the prefixes. One has been done for you.

1. illegible

Answer: illegible

2. impossible

3. illegal

4. irresponsible

5. inactive

6. impatient

7. intolerant

8. immobile

Try these

Copy these root words, then add the prefixes –**in**, –**ir**, –**im** or –**il**. One has been done for you.

1. convenient

   Answer: *inconvenient*

2. correct
3. capable
4. literate
5. responsible
6. competent
7. proper

Now try these

Copy and complete the sentences by choosing the correct spelling for each word. One has been done for you.

1. Akhil's skiing holiday was ________. (incredible / imcredible)

   Answer: *Akhil's skiing holiday was incredible.*

2. Antonia found the chocolate cake ________! (imresistable / irresistible)
3. Christopher's handwriting was ________. (illegible / inlegible)
4. My brother can be so childish and ________. (inmature / immature)
5. I got five ________ answers in my maths test. (incorrect / uncorrect)

The prefixes re– and inter–

Prefixes change the meaning of the root word. The prefix **re–** means **again**. The prefix **inter–** means **between** or **among**. When you add **re–** or **inter–** to a word, you do not have to make any changes to the root word.

Get started

Copy the words and then underline the prefix in each word. One has been done for you.

1. interview

   Answer: interview

2. rename
3. rewrite
4. redo
5. interlink
6. international
7. interaction
8. react

Try these

Copy the words, then add the prefix **re–** or **inter–**. One has been done for you.

1. value

Answer: *revalue*

2. locate

3. national

4. assemble

5. dial

6. claim

7. unite

8. deliver

Now try these

Copy and complete the sentences by adding the correct prefix. One has been done for you.

1. It was busy at Exeter ____national Airport today.

Answer: *It was busy at Exeter International Airport today.*

2. Mo waited for the rainbow to ____appear.

3. I need to do lots of ____vision for my exams.

4. It was a long, slow ____city bus journey.

5. Today I am going to ____organise my desk.

6. The Johnsons want to ____locate to a new area.

The prefixes sub- and super-

A prefix is a group of letters that you can add to the start of a root word. The prefix **sub–** means **under** or **less than**. The prefix **super–** means **above** or **more than**. When you add **sub–** or **super–** to a root word, you do not change the spelling of the root word.

Get started

Copy these words and underline the prefixes in each word. One has been done for you.

1. supermarket

   Answer: <u>super</u>market

2. submarine
3. superstar
4. subway
5. superhuman
6. superstore
7. subtract
8. subscribe

Try these

Copy the root words then add the prefix **sub–** or **super–**. One has been done for you.

1. title

   Answer: *subtitle*

2. heading
3. divide
4. section
5. size
6. man
7. vision
8. merge

Now try these

Copy and complete the sentences by writing the missing prefix. One has been done for you.

1. The new ____market opened last week.

   Answer: *The new supermarket opened last week.*

2. The atmosphere at the match was ____dued.
3. He lifted the car with ____human strength.
4. Never use sharp knives without ____vision.
5. Janice cancelled her ____scription to the magazine.
6. The submariners lived aboard their ____marine.

The prefixes anti- and auto-

A prefix is a group of letters added to the start of a root word. The prefix **anti–** is used to mean **against**. The prefix **auto–** is used to mean **self** or **own**.

Get started

Copy these words then underline the prefixes. One has been done for you.

1. automatic

   Answer: <u>auto</u>matic
2. anticlockwise
3. antiseptic
4. automobile
5. antisocial
6. antibiotics

Try these

Copy the root words then add the prefix **anti–** or **auto–**. One has been done for you.

1. graph

   Answer: *autograph*

2. climax
3. pilot
4. freeze
5. hero
6. clockwise

Now try these

Copy and complete the sentences by writing the missing prefixes. One has been done for you.

1. For some spider bites there is no ____ dote.

   Answer: *For some spider bites there is no antidote.*

2. The band signed ____graphs as they left the concert.
3. Littering and drawing graffiti are ____social activities.
4. What a life she has led! She should write an ____biography.
5. I cleaned his cuts and grazes with ____bacterial wipes.
6. The end of the film was a disappointing ____climax.

Review unit 1

Can you remember the spellings you've learned? Answer these questions to find out.

A. Add the suffix or prefix to each word. Remember, sometimes you will need to double the last letter before adding the suffix.

1. number + ed
2. admit + ed
3. target + ing
4. begin + er
5. re + write
6. inter + national
7. re + name
8. re + place
9. anti + clockwise
10. auto + pilot
11. super + market
12. sub + level

B. Choose the correct spelling of each word.

1. mith / myth
2. pyramid / piramyd
3. cristyl / crystal
4. Egypt / Egipt
5. cousin / cusin
6. touch / tuch
7. duble / double
8. trouble / truble

C. Use the prefixes **dis–**, **mis–**, **il–**, **im–**, **in–** and **ir–** to write the opposites of these words.

1. appear

2. obey

3. spell

4. understand

5. legal

6. possible

7. correct

8. regular

The suffix -ation

A suffix is a group of letters added to the end of a root word. The suffix **–ation** turns verbs into nouns. If the verb ends in an **e**, remove the **e** before adding **–ation**.

Get started

Copy and complete the chart. Write words from the list that are spelt correctly in the first column. Correct the spelling of the other words and write them in the second column.

1. formation
2. continuation
3. sensation
4. continueation
5. senseation
6. admireation
7. determineation
8. admiration

Correctly spelt words	Corrected words
formation	

Try these

Copy these verbs and turn them into nouns by adding **–ation**. One has been done for you.

1. limit

   Answer: *limitation*

2. inspire
3. explore
4. observe
5. compile
6. reserve

Now try these

Copy and complete the sentences by adding **–ation** to one verb in each sentence. Underline the word you change. One has been done for you.

1. The children read the inform on the poster.

   Answer: *The children read the information on the poster.*

2. Rahul was full of admire for his hero.
3. Carl made a reserve at the restaurant.
4. Anika makes an observe of rare birds.
5. We should support the conserve of wildlife.
6. Oscar studied hard in prepare for his exams.

Adding the suffix -ly to words ending with y

If you add the suffix **–ly** to an adjective, you can turn it into an adverb. Normally, you can add **–ly** to a root word without changing the spelling. However, if the root word ends with **y** and is longer than one syllable, you must change the final **y** into an **i** before you add **–ly**.

Get started

Copy these words, then underline the suffix **–ly**. One has been done for you.

1. sleepily

   Answer: *sleepily*
2. prettily
3. breezily
4. cheekily
5. messily
6. shakily
7. angrily
8. hungrily

Try these

Copy the root words, then add the suffix **–ly**. One has been done for you.

1. nasty

   Answer: *nastily*
2. hasty
3. ready
4. grumpy
5. busy
6. easy

Now try these

Copy and complete these sentences by choosing the correct spelling. One has been done for you.

1. The man tucked into the hamburger ____________. (hungrily / hungryly)

   Answer: *The man tucked into the hamburger hungrily.*
2. The visitor was dressed____________. (shabbily / shabbly)
3. The boy wrote ____________ on the form. (shakly / shakily)
4. The man walked to his car____________. (happily / happyly)
5. The thief left the building ____________. (hastily / hastly)
6. The racing car zoomed ____________ around the corner. (noisely / noisily)

The ending -sure

The buzzy **/zhur/** sound at the end of words is spelt **sure**.

Get started

Say the words below aloud and listen to the **/zhur/** sound. Copy them and underline the letters that stand for the **/zhur/** sound. One has been done for you.

1. treasure

   Answer: *trea<u>sure</u>*

2. leisure
3. closure
4. pleasure
5. enclosure
6. measure
7. exposure
8. disclosure

Try these

Correct the spelling errors in each word. One has been done for you.

1. compozure

   Answer: *composure*

2. displeashure
3. expozure
4. leishure
5. clozure
6. disclosuer

Now try these

Use the words below in sentences of your own. One has been done for you.

1. enclosure

   Answer: *Bess fed the puppies in the enclosure.*

2. measure
3. treasure
4. displeasure
5. leisure
6. pleasure

The ending -ture

Words that end with a /**cher**/ sound often have the letter pattern **–ture**.

Remember, the /**cher**/ sound at the end of a word can also be spelt **cher** or **tcher**, for example: ri**cher**, tea**cher**, ca**tcher** and stre**tcher**.

Get started

Copy the words then underline the /**cher**/ sound. One has been done for you.

1. furniture

   Answer: *furni<u>ture</u>*
2. capture
3. vulture
4. creature
5. nature
6. adventure
7. puncture
8. rupture

Try these

Correct the spelling mistakes in the list below. One has been done for you.

1. piccher

   Answer: *picture*

2. moistcher
3. temperacher
4. futuer
5. fractcher
6. postior

Now try these

Use the words below in sentences of your own. One has been done for you.

1. creature

   Answer: *Bears are woodland creatures.*

2. nature
3. capture
4. picture
5. adventure
6. pastures

The ending -sion

The buzzy /**zhun**/ sound at the end of words is often spelt **–sion**.

Get started

Copy the words and underline the /**zhun**/ sound. One has been done for you.

1. television

   Answer: *televi<u>sion</u>*

2. division
3. vision
4. confusion
5. invasion
6. decision
7. explosion
8. provision

Try these

Choose the correct spelling for each word. One has been done for you.

1. illution / illusion

   Answer: *illusion*

2. revision / revission
3. conclution / conclusion
4. occasion / occastion
5. collission / collision
6. version / vershun

Now try these

Use the words below in sentences of your own. One has been done for you.

1. confusion

   Answer: *There was confusion over school opening times.*

2. division
3. illusion
4. conclusion
5. revision
6. collision
7. invasion

The suffix -ous

Many adjectives end with the suffix **–ous**.

Add the suffix **–ous** to the end of the root word.

If the root word ends with **e**, like fam**e**, you normally drop the **e** before adding **–ous**.

If the root word ends with a soft /**j**/ sound, you keep the final **e**.

If the root word ends with **y**, like var**y**, you change **y** to **i** before adding **–ous**.

If the root word ends with **–our,** you change **–our** to **–or** before adding the **–ous**.

Sometimes there is not a clear root word.

If there is an /**ee**/ sound before the **–ous,** it is normally spelt with an **i.** However, sometimes this /**ee**/ sound is spelt with an **e**.

Get started

Copy the words and underline the suffix **–ous**. One has been done for you.

1. ravenous

Answer: *raven<u>ous</u>*

2. poisonous

3. fabulous

4. nervous

5. ridiculous

6. hazardous

Try these

Add the **–ous** ending to these words. Write the new words. Remember, you might need to change the root word before you add the ending. One has been done for you.

1. vary

   Answer: *various*

2. courage
3. humour
4. advantage
5. prosper
6. fame
7. adventure

Now try these

Use the words below in sentences of your own. One has been done for you.

1. curious

   Answer: *Cats have a reputation for being curious.*

2. dangerous
3. glamorous
4. mountainous
5. hideous
6. nervous

The endings -tion, -sion, -ssion and -cian

There are different ways of spelling the /**shun**/ sound: **–tion**, **–sion**, **–ssion** and **–cian**.

The most common way of spelling the /**shun**/ sound is **–tion**. Use this when the root word ends in **t** or **te**.

For root words ending in **–ss** or **–mit**, spell the /**shun**/ sound **–ssion**.

If the root word ends in **te**, like comple**te**, drop the final **e** before adding **–ion**.

For root words ending in **d** or a consonant then **se**, spell the /**shun**/ sound **–sion**. If the root word ends in **d**, like exten**d**, drop the **d** before adding **–sion**.

For root words ending in **c** or **cs**, spell the /**shun**/ sound **–cian**. If the root word ends in **cs**, drop the final **s** before adding **–ian**.

Get started

Copy the words then underline the different ways of spelling the /**shun**/ sound. One has been done for you.

1. discussion

Answer: *discussion*

2. musician

3. percussion

4. action

5. tension

6. admission

7. election

Try these

Choose the correct spelling of the /**shun**/ sound for each word. One has been done for you.

1. invenssion / invension / invention

   Answer: *invention*

2. politission / politician / politision
3. injection / injecssion / injecsion
4. magition / magission / magician
5. eruption / erupcian / erupsion
6. perfeccian / perfection / perfecsion

Now try these

Copy and complete the sentences by adding the correct suffix to the underlined words. One has been done for you.

1. Rover the dog knew the <u>direct</u> home.

   Answer: *Rover the dog knew the direction home.*

2. The Mayor worried about the coming <u>elect</u>.
3. My sister is a very talented <u>music</u>.
4. I can recite the alphabet without <u>hesitate</u>.
5. Football is Cynthia's growing <u>obsess</u>.
6. It is important to get a good <u>educate</u>.

The /k/ sound spelt ch

There are several ways of spelling the /**k**/ sound. In some words the /**k**/ sound is spelt **ch**.

For example:

- a**ch**e
- **ch**aracter

Get started

Copy these words and underline the letters that stand for the /**k**/ sound. One has been done for you.

1. headache

   Answer: *headache*
2. chemist
3. chorus
4. scheme
5. stomach
6. school
7. chord
8. mechanic

Try these

Copy the sentences then underline the words in which the /**k**/ sound is spelt **ch**. One has been done for you.

1. Tom's stomach hurt from eating too much cheese.

   Answer: *Tom's stomach hurt from eating too much cheese.*

2. Cherries always give me tummy ache.
3. Charles called out and his voice made an echo.
4. The school rabbit was munching a carrot.
5. The room was in chaos, but Gran still looked cheery.

Now try these

Copy and complete the sentences by choosing the correct spelling of the words. One has been done for you.

1. Nina was looking forward to the ______________ disco. (skool / school)

   Answer: *Nina was looking forward to the school disco.*

2. We went to the ______________ with my aunt. (market / marchet)
3. Flavia plays the saxophone in our town ______________. (orchestra / orkestra)
4. The ______________ old lady had made a cake. (chind / kind)
5. We made the ______________ such a mess! (kitchen / chitchen)

The /sh/ sound spelt ch

In most words, the /**sh**/ sound is spelt as it is said, with the letters **sh** as in **sh**ower.

However, in some words the /**sh**/ sound is spelt with the letters **ch** as in **ch**ef.

Get started

Copy and complete the chart by sorting these words into two groups: those with the /**sh**/ sound spelt **sh**, and those with the /**sh**/ sound spelt **ch**. One has been done for you.

1. moustache
2. chef
3. ship
4. machine
5. fashion
6. chalet
7. brochure
8. dish

/**sh**/ spelt **ch**	/**sh**/ spelt **sh**
moustache	

Try these

Copy and complete the words by using the letters **ch** or **sh**. One has been done for you.

1. _ _andelier

   Answer: *chandelier*

2. ca_ _ ier
3. qui_ _e
4. a_ _amed
5. sa_ _et
6. cu_ _ion

Now try these

Copy and complete the sentences by choosing the correct spelling. One has been done for you.

1. The __________ floated safely to the ground. (parachutist / parashutist)

   Answer: *The parachutist floated safely to the ground.*

2. I don't really care about following __________. (fachion / fashion)
3. The meal was cooked by an excellent __________. (chef / shef)
4. I like a __________ topping on my pizza. (muchroom / mushroom)
5. I have a __________ every day. (chower / shower)

Review unit 2

Can you remember the spellings you've learned? Carry out these activities to find out.

A. Write down the correct spelling of each words.

1. measher / measure
2. pleashure / pleasure
3. adventure / advencher
4. creacher / creature
5. future / fuchure
6. nacher / nature
7. televishon / television
8. nervous / nerveous
9. discushon / discussion
10. headake / headache
11. stomach / stomack
12. mashine / machine

B. Add the suffixes to the words. Remember, you might need to change the ending of the original word before you add the suffix.

1. explore + ation
2. inspire + ation
3. prepare + ation
4. busy + ly
5. happy + ly
6. noisy + ly

C. Write the sentences and complete the missing word in each sentence.

1. The pirates used a map to find the tr _________ buried on the island.
2. Joe painted a pic ______ of his granny.
3. Toni had a very difficult dec _______ to make: strawberry or chocolate ice cream.
4. In all the confu ______ at the end of the party, Suzy forgot her coat.
5. The inven ______ of the internet has changed our lives.
6. Mrs Mason's hat was so ridic _______, we couldn't stop laughing.
7. The musi ______ s playing in the market square cheered us up.
8. We all joined in with the c _______ of the song.
9. I love cooking. I want to be a ____ f when I grow up.
10. The glam _______ film star walked down the red carpet.

The sound /k/ spelt -que and the sound /g/ spelt -gue

In some words, the /**k**/ sound is spelt **–que**. In some words, the /**g**/ sound is spelt **–gue**.

Get started

Copy and complete the chart by sorting these words into two groups: words where /**k**/ is spelt **–que** and words where /**g**/ is spelt **–gue**. One has been done for you.

1. arabesque
2. antique
3. cheque
4. tongue
5. rogue
6. league
7. boutique
8. meringue

/**k**/ spelt **–que**	/**g**/ spelt **–gue**
arabesque	

Try these

Copy and complete the words by adding **–que** or **–gue**. One has been done for you.

1. ton_ _ _

   Answer: *tongue*

2. lea _ _ _
3. anti _ _ _
4. ro _ _ _
5. bouti _ _ _

Now try these

Copy and complete the sentences by choosing the correct spelling. One has been done for you.

1. The film about sharks contained very little __________. (dialogue / dialoque)

   Answer: *The film about sharks contained very little dialogue.*

2. The Normans __________ England in 1066. (conguered / conquered)
3. The millionaire signed a large __________. (chegue / cheque)
4. The Great __________ was also known as the Black Death. (Plague / Plaque)
5. We had to __________ for ages at the supermarket. (gueue / queue)

The sound /s/ spelt sc

There are different ways of spelling the /**s**/ sound. One way to spell it is **sc**.

Get started

Copy and complete the chart by sorting these words into two groups: words where /**s**/ is spelt **sc** and words where /**s**/ is spelt **s** or **c**. One has been done for you.

1. song
2. descend
3. decent
4. scene
5. seen
6. scent
7. sent
8. crescent

/**s**/ spelt **sc**	/**s**/ spelt **s** or **c**
	song

Try these

Copy the words and underline **sc** in each word. One has been done for you.

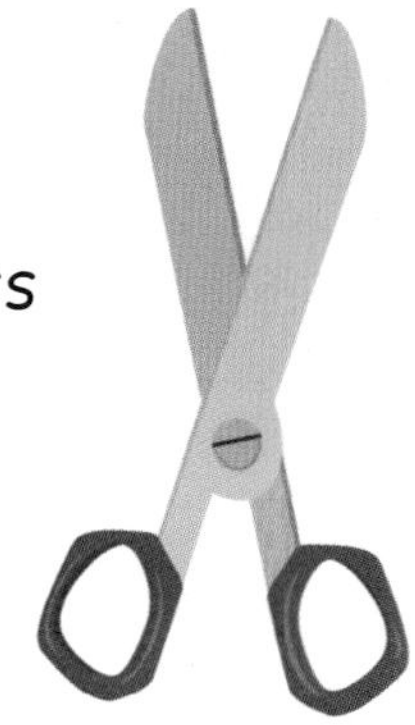

1. scissors

   Answer: <u>sc</u>issors
2. descend
3. abscess
4. scent
5. scenery
6. fascinate

Now try these

Use the words below in sentences of your own. You may use a dictionary if you need to. The first one has been done for you.

1. scenic

   Answer: Helen and Andrew walked a scenic route.
2. muscles
3. crescent
4. scent
5. science

The sound /ay/ spelt ei, eigh and ey

There are lots of different ways of spelling the /**ay**/ sound. Three ways to spell the sound /**ay**/ are with the letters **ei**, **eigh** or **ey**.

Get started

Copy and complete the chart by sorting these words into three groups: words where /**ay**/ is spelt **ei**, words where /**ay**/ is spelt **eigh** and words where /**ay**/ is spelt **ey**. One has been done for you.

1. beige
2. eighteen
3. weightlifter
4. convey
5. neighbourhood
6. paperweight
7. survey
8. prey

/**ay**/ spelt **ei**	/**ay**/ spelt **eigh**	/**ay**/ spelt **ey**
beige		

Try these

Copy these words then underline the letters that are used for the /**ay**/ sound in each word. One has been done for you.

1. eight

   Answer: *eight*
2. obey
3. sleigh
4. veil
5. eighty

Now try these

Copy and complete the sentences by choosing the correct spelling. One has been done for you.

1. The lion stalks its __________. (prei / preigh / prey)

   Answer: *The lion stalks its prey.*
2. Hamid's alarm clock rang at __________ o'clock. (eit / eight / eyt)
3. The old man had a __________ beard. (grei / greigh / grey)
4. The King's __________ lasted many years. (rein / reighn / reyn)
5. Blood runs through our __________. (veins / veighns / veyns)

The possessive apostrophe with plural words

To show that something belongs to more than one person or thing, use a possessive apostrophe after the plural form of the noun to which the thing belongs. If the word already ends in **s**, only add the apostrophe. If it doesn't end in **s**, add an **s** after the apostrophe.

Some singular proper nouns (names of people and places) already end in **s**. For these words, add another **s** after the apostrophe.

Get started

Copy the two columns of words and then match each singular word with its plural. One has been done for you.

1. *girl*	**a)** puppies
2. cat	**b)** men
3. child	**c)** geese
4. lorry	**d)** cats
5. puppy	**e)** lorries
6. chair	**f)** *girls*
7. man	**g)** children
8. goose	**h)** chairs

Try these

Decide whether the underlined word in each sentence is singular or plural. One has been done for you.

1. The puppies' toys were chewed.

   Answer: *plural*

2. The goose's egg was golden.
3. The cat's food was in the bowl.
4. The men's coats were warm.
5. The girls' hairbands were white.

Now try these

Copy and complete the sentences with the correct use of the possessive apostrophe. One has been done for you.

1. Chloe held on tightly to the __________ leads. (puppy's / puppies')

   Answer: *Chloe held on tightly to the puppies' leads.*

2. The __________ covers were worn. (books' / book's)
3. The __________ boots were waterproof. (women's / womens's)
4. __________favourite drink was milkshake. (James's / Jame's)
5. Khalid stayed at his__________ house. (friends' / friend's)

Homophones and near-homophones (1)

Homophones are words that sound the same but are spelt differently and have different meanings.

Get started

Put the words into homophone pairs. One has been done for you.

bury	accept	medal	except	who's	effect
berry	meddle	affect	weather	whether	whose

Answer: *bury, berry*

Copy and complete the definitions with words from the list. One has been done for you.

1. __________: a small juicy fruit

   Answer: *berry: a small juicy fruit*

2. __________: a contraction of the words **who** and **is** or **has**
3. __________: belonging to
4. __________: to interfere or tinker
5. __________: not including
6. __________: put in a hole and cover with earth

Try these

Copy the list of words and add the homophones. One has been done for you.

1. medal

   Answer: *medal, meddle*

2. except
3. who's
4. effect
5. bury

Now try these

Copy and complete the sentences by choosing the correct homophone. One has been done for you.

1. The _________ was good for the school trip. (whether / weather)

   Answer: *The weather was good for the school trip.*

2. Samira _________ the party invitation. (accepted / excepted)
3. Squirrels love to _________ nuts in the garden. (bury / berry)
4. Jack proudly showed off his swimming _________. (medal / meddle)
5. I bought a cake with a _________ on top. (bury / berry)

Homophones and near-homophones (2)

Homophones are words that sound the same but are spelt differently and have different meanings.

Get started

Put the words into homophone pairs. One has been done for you.

hear	he'll	grate	grown	here	great
heal	knot	heel	groan	not	

Answer: *heal, heel*

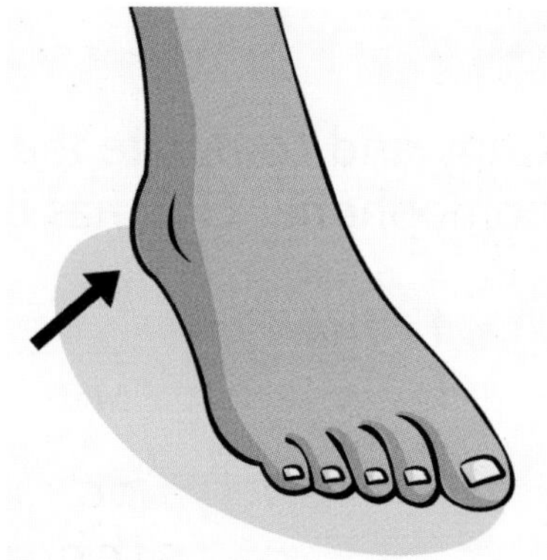

Copy and complete the definitions. One has been done for you.

1. _____: the back of the foot

   Answer: *heel: the back of the foot*

2. _____: a contraction of the words **he** and **will**
3. _____: to become healthy again
4. _____: when something has become larger
5. _____: a noise of pain or despair

Try these

Copy the list of words and add the homophones. One has been done for you.

1. great

   Answer: *great, grate*

2. grown
3. heel
4. knot
5. hear

Now try these

Copy and complete the sentences by choosing the correct homophone. One has been done for you.

1. Dogs can __________ very high-pitched sounds. (hear / here)

   Answer: *Dogs can hear very high-pitched sounds.*

2. Tessa let out a __________ at the awful joke. (groan / grown)
3. The sailor was glad he could tie so many__________. (knots / nots)
4. The cut on Majid's finger would not __________. (heel / he'll / heal)
5. The new shoes hurt Sheila's __________. (heal / he'll / heel)

Homophones and near-homophones (3)

Homophones are words that sound the same but are spelt differently and have different meanings.

Get started

Put the words into homophone pairs.
One has been done for you.

mist	plane	fair	missed
mane	peace	meat	plain
main	meet	fare	piece

Answer: *meet, meat*

Copy and complete the definitions with words from the list. One has been done for you.

1. ________: long hair on a horse's or lion's neck

   Answer: *mane: long hair on a horse's or lion's neck*

2. ________: a wide, flat level surface
3. ________: simple, basic or without decoration
4. ________: tiny drops of water in the air
5. ________: a part of something
6. ________: the amount you pay to travel on a train
7. ________: the flesh of animals
8. ________: a state of calm or quiet

Try these

Copy the correctly spelt words in each set. Some have more than one. One has been done for you.

1. plain   plaine   plane

   Answer: *plain, plane*

2. peace   peece   peaze
3. missed   myst   mist
4. meit   miet   meet
5. peese   piece   peice
6. fare   fair   fayer

Now try these

Copy and complete the sentences by choosing the correct spelling of the words. One has been done for you.

1. The horse's __________ was brushed for the show. (main / mane)

   Answer: *The horse's mane was brushed for the show.*

2. The damp __________ rose from the river. (missed / mist)
3. The wind swept across the grassy __________. (plain / plane)
4. Jamil found the last __________ of the jigsaw. (peace / piece)
5. I went on all the scary rides at the __________. (fair / fare)

Homophones and near-homophones (4)

Homophones are words that sound the same but are spelt differently and have different meanings.

Get started

Put the words into homophone pairs. One has been done for you.

ball	brake	male	break	mail	rain	scene	seen	bawl	rein

Answer: *male, mail*

Copy and complete the definitions with words from the list. One has been done for you.

1. __________: letters and parcels

   Answer: *mail: letters and parcels*

2. __________: water falling from the sky
3. __________: a strap for guiding horses
4. __________: to cry loudly

Try these

Copy the list of words and add the homophones. One has been done for you.

1. rain

   Answer: *rain, rein*

2. ball
3. seen
4. scene
5. break

Now try these

Copy and complete the sentences by choosing the correct spelling of the words. One has been done for you.

1. Tariq was determined to __________ all his racing records. (brake / break)

   Answer: *Tariq was determined to break all his racing records.*

2. A __________ sheep is called a ram. (mail / male)
3. It was the biggest cake I had ever __________. (scene / seen)
4. The __________ were made of leather. (rains / reigns / reins)
5. To stop the car, press down on the __________. (brake / break)

Review unit 3

Can you remember the spellings you've learned? Carry out these activities to find out.

A. Look at each picture and write the word.

1. 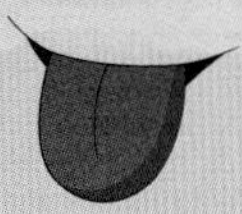 t _ _ _ _ _

2.  q _ _ _ _

3. 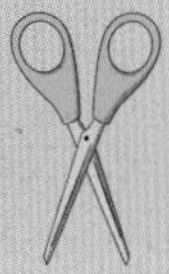 s _ _ _ _ _ _ _

4.  m _ _ _ _ _ _ s

5.  e _ _ _ _

6.  n _ _ _ _ bour

B. Copy and complete the sentences, correctly adding the missing apostrophes.

1. The bunnies ears were fluffy.
2. Both tables legs were wobbly.
3. Tonys house is just down the road from mine.
4. The swimmers teeth were chattering after their swim in the sea.
5. We stayed at the waters edge and paddled.
6. After two days rest, the hikers were ready to start walking again.

C. Copy and complete the sentences, writing the missing words.

1. Guess w_____ coming to stay tomorrow!
2. Everyone e_____t Josh can go and get their coats.
3. M_____s were hung round the necks of the children who came first, second and third.
4. "Oh no! Not cabbage!" gr_____ed Ruby and Cavan.
5. Sadly, my new boots rub and have given me a blister on my h_____l.
6. It was a foggy day and soon we were lost in the m_____.
7. Can you m_____t me by the clock tower?
8. Come and see me after the lunch br_____ and I will help you.
9. You must ob _____ the safety rules at the adventure park.
10. We checked the _____t of our bags before we left for the airport.